The Book Of Self:

Love, Care, Esteem, and Worth

Garicka Jackson

HerLife HerWrite Publishing Co. LLC

ISBN: 978-1-7349232-2-3

Table of Contents

SELF LOVE

"Love yourself girl or nobody will"

-J.Cole

Introduction

Did you know that there are 8 types of love one can express? There is philia, pragma, storge, eros, ludas, mania, philautia, and agape. Of those 8 types of love, the most important one is philautia, meaning self-love, according to *FTD by Designs*.

Self-love is the most important because our body is a temple. We must nourish, love, and take care of our body. Self love is also important because it lays the foundations for self care, self esteem, and self worth. Self love is believing that we are worthy of love, respect, belonging, and safety regardless of how we think, feel, and act at the moment. Your belief of being worthy should be unshakeable despite your feelings in the present moment.

As we know, love it's not just a noun and emotion, it's also a verb. Love requires action and must be worked at consistently. Self love requires that same action. You must show up for yourself every day and be committed to doing so, even when you feel undeserving of it. We show self love through action by giving ourselves love and respect. This is done by giving ourselves love and respect, respecting our minds, body, heart, and time. A few ways to respect your, mind, body, and time is:

- 💜 Don't let other people's opinions about you, control how you view yourself. (yourself)
- 💜 Don't speak badly too or about yourself (mind)
- 💜 Don't let anybody force you to be something or do something just for their friendship or approval. (yourself)
- 💜 Don't go against your morals (mind, yourself, body)
- 💜 Control your emotions (mind)
- 💜 Setting and maintaining boundaries (time)
- 💜 Be responsible, do things that need to be done. (time)

Before we dig deeper into self love we're going to do a self-love journaling exercise. As you continue on through this book you will find several journal activities for you that correspond with the section. Answer each question and remember to always be honest with yourself when answering any of the questions in this book. The only way to have a positive and accurate outcome is to be openly honest with yourself. On the following page, you will find your first journaling activity for self love.

Self Love Journaling

In your own words define self love?

Why do you believe it is important to love yourself?

Make a list of the things and people you love. Use at least 5 people and 5 things, placing what you love the most at the top and least at the bottom.

♥

♥

♥

♥

♥

♥

♥

♥

♥

♥

Read over your list.

How long did it take you to list yourself as one of the people you love?

Did you even list yourself at all?

List 3 qualities that you love about yourself:

♥

♥

♥

List 5 reasons to love yourself:

♥

♥

♥

♥

♥

List 5 ways you show love to yourself:

❤

❤

❤

❤

❤

"In order to love who you are you cannot hate the experiences that shaped you"

-Andrea Dykstra

Loving Yourself

When you take a look in your mirror, what do you see? *A reflection;* Not just any reflection, it's yours. How you view this reflection is the most important key in SELF LOVE. I remember looking in the mirror analyzing and comparing my figure to what society perceives as beauty. I didn't feel pretty, at all. I felt as though I was a foreigner trapped inside of a body I was no longer comfortable with. I gave so much love to those around me that I began to strip the love that I gave myself.

Self love is the beginning of all things beautiful. It's extremely hard to love someone else, without loving yourself first. You will not be able to love anyone else properly or receive genuine love until you've experienced the love that can surface from within. Loving you, teaches you how to love others. I know you're tired of *treating others how you want to be treated,* but self love is exactly that in reverse. TREAT YOURSELF HOW YOU WOULD WANT OTHERS TO TREAT YOU. Loving me was the best decision I have ever made, it's refreshing as well as good for the mind, body, and soul. YOU should be your number one priority.

The road to self love isn't easy especially if you've dealt with verbal abuse, insecurities, colorism, sexual abuse, comparison, emotional abuse, bullying, and so many other things. Self love is a journey that is not often easy, but you don't have to take the road alone. Falling in love with yourself again is not something that is going to happen overnight. You will have to work at it day after day for the rest of your life. After all Rome wasn't built in a day. Yes, it is okay to care and give love to everyone else, but let's stop neglecting ourselves while we are doing so. I am still learning to love myself daily. Some days I feel like I have the whole world in my hands and my confidence is at its peak; on others I feel like I'm struggling to stay above the surface. This is not an easy battle, but it is a battle worth fighting.

It is important to give yourself love so that you know what genuine love feels like. You won't put up with any bullshit from someone loving you halfway. While learning to love yourself, you begin to discover new things about yourself that you were once blind too. Take the time to get to know you, date yourself, and surround yourself with positive energy and positive people. The biggest factor to self love is being kind to yourself, placing high vibrating vibes into the atmosphere, killing comparisons, being body positive, gaining confidence, and continuing to stride with your head held high despite the opinions of others. We will conquer self love through self care, self esteem, and self worth. As stated before self love sets the foundation for self care, self esteem, and self worth. If you don't love yourself you will not care for yourself properly in the emotional, mental, and physical aspects. Your self esteem will be low and your worth will be questioned.

The first transition into loving ourselves will be through self care. Self care is first because in my opinion, it also helps lead up to self esteem and self worth. So, before we can move along to building the love we have for ourselves through self esteem and self worth, we have to demonstrate our love through how we choose to take care of ourselves. If we don't take care of ourselves, how are we going to take care of others? If you don't take care of yourself then who will? If you don't take the time to learn to love yourself, you will:

- Settle for anyone
- Allow anything
- Be easily manipulated
- Have low self-esteem
- Constantly comparing yourself

- And will conform to fit in with society

Before transitioning into our next step in *The Book of Self*, we are going to end it with a self love activity called, "all about me." In this exercise, you will answer a numerous number of questions on the topic of you. You can't fall in love with yourself without knowing what you love the most, getting to know yourself, finding room for self improvement, and much more. Take this time to answer these questions with full honesty. No one sees anything you write unless you allow them too.

All about Me, Myself, and I

My best personality trait(s):

My biggest fear:

My biggest regret:

My greatest accomplishments:

Who is my role model and why?

I would date me because:

What I love most about me?

What makes me feel loved?

What do I look for when I love others?

Insecurities I have hidden:

Favorite things to do:

Most validated reason that I love myself:

On a scale of 1-10, my self esteem is:

How often do I schedule a day to myself?

If I could change one thing it would be:

One thing I would never change about myself:

Five positive things I can say about myself:

- ❤
- ❤
- ❤
- ❤
- ❤

One thing I've done that I'm proud of myself for:

Best physical feature:

What inspires me?

Song to describe my life:

Favorite song when I'm feeling down:

If I had more courage, I would do _____ differently in my life.

What is good about my living right now?

If I could eliminate one weakness in my life, it would be?

My strengths:

Do I prefer people to be straight forward or tempered with me?

Most embarrassing moment:

Favorite swear word:

Favorite thing to say to myself:

Something I look for in a partner:

How difficult is it for me to forgive?

How difficult is it to be honest with myself?

During difficult times, would I rather be alone or surrounded by friends?

One thing I'd pay somebody to do rather than do it myself?

Last compliment I received was:

Guilty pleasure that I enjoy too much to give up:

One thing that I hope never changes:

What drains my energy?

How do I replenish my energy?

Most difficult thing I've done for love:

Pettiest thing I've done to prove a point:

One thing I won't do for love:

Describe myself in three words:

- ♥

- ♥

- ♥

Three things that draw me to someone:

- ♥

- ♥

- ♥

What's something that is unforgivable?

Some things most people don't know about me:

What do I think about more than anything else?

How does music matter to me?

If I could give my younger self advice, what would it be?

If I could fix one relationship which one would it be? Why?

I forgive myself for:

5 things that make me happy:

- ❤
- ❤
- ❤
- ❤
- ❤

What aspects of myself do I need to show more love to?

What's the first thing you look at when you meet a person? Why?

(On these questions, specify the reason you chose the answer that you did.)

Summer or winter:

Spring or fall:

Valentine's Day or Halloween:

Text or phone call:

Half empty or half full:

Cats or dog:

Amusement Park or Water Park:

Super strong or super smart:

Chicken, Beef or neither:

Forgiveness or revenge:

Turn the other cheek or I need my lick back:

Cash or card:

Natural or makeup:

Ponytail or bun:

Straight or curly:

Soda or pop:

Thunder or lightning:

Pencil or pen:

East coast or west coast:

Comedy or drama:

Horror or thriller:

In this next section, we will begin our journey to self love with self care. Self care, according to Oxford English Dictionary, *is the practice of taking an active role in protecting one's own well-being and happiness, in particular during periods of stress*. Sometimes we can get so busy taking care of others that we forget to take care of ourselves, and sometimes we can just be too busy in general. In addition to that, we can be stressed unknowingly and that takes a toll on our body and mental health. We have to learn to stop neglecting ourselves. Hopefully, this will help us begin our process in self-care, the first step in loving ourselves.

SELF CARE

"Self care is giving the world the best of you instead of what's left of you."

-Katie Reed

Introduction

The first step to self love is self care. You cannot do anything on a low battery. Take some time to recharge before you hop back into your everyday routine. Sometimes sleep alone is not enough to recharge, so make some time to really give yourself a break from everything. It's not selfish to put yourself first, its self love. Self care comes in many forms and is different for everyone. Self care is:

- Saying "no" when your plate is too full. You aren't obligated to do things for others. Know your limit to things and don't exceed it. You will wear yourself thin if you continue to do things for others and never make time for yourself.

- A nice warm bubble bath after a long day. SOAK away that stress, Sis! Throw on some slow jams, pour you a glass of wine, and a face mask. It will have you walking out of the bathroom feeling like a new woman, and possibly a bit tipsy.

- Blunt and book. Get lifted and lost in that book you keep saying you're going to start *"Tomorrow."* Today was tomorrow on yesterday... What's taking you so long?

- A date with yourself... You don't need anyone else around to enjoy yourself. Grow comfortable with taking yourself out and enjoying your own company.

- Date with friends, whether it's a girl's night out or in. Throwing ass while your friends scream "AYEE" is self care. lol

- Doing something you enjoy! Make time for the things you used to love, but had to put on the backburner.

- Doing something new, go ahead and knock a few things off that bucket list that has been collecting dust. DO IT, I DARE YOU.

- Spending time alone. Again, you don't have to be in the presence of others to have a good time. Everyone needs time alone every once in a while. Cook one of those many meals you have pinned to Pinterest for once.

- Taking you out to eat. Don't pay attention to anyone around you or do! Go out to eat, order your favorite meal, and people watch. You will be surprised by how relaxing this is.

- A day without social media!!! Social media can be draining, give your mind a break from the drama.

- Making sure you're mentally in a good space. It is an important key to self care and self love. (Don't be afraid during this journey because you will start to realize that some people in your life are holding you down and their energies affect you negatively. This journey won't be easy so surround yourself with people who have the same common goals and attitude as you. Everyone does not deserve your time, but the people you do let in need to be those who have a positive aura and want to better themselves as well as others.

- Painting or drawing. Draw out your mood, something silly, and something that makes you happy. Whatever it is let the pencil or paintbrush consume you.

- Yoga and Meditation. NOW THIS is relaxation and re-centering. You'll begin to feel the calmness overtake your body and can tell a difference when you go without it after being in a routine. Yoga helps balance your chakras and get your emotions in check. There is a section further along that explains the positives of yoga and aligning your chakras. It helped me gain control of a lot more within my life and find peace within myself.

- Exercise. Take a walk alone, a dance class, ride your bike, go window shopping and get them steps in!

- Retail Therapy. Hop off that couch and stop clicking that mouse, or screen! Get out and shop til' you drop (Just make sure you don't hurt your pockets too much).

- Long shower and fresh shave

- Keeping up your hygiene

- Parked car conversation. Now, I don't know about you, but something about venting and talking about any and everything that comes to mind is freeing.

- Take a self defense class. So many times a woman feels powerless and self defense classes can really empower someone.

- Self expression is a form of self care. Speak up for yourself, be vocal and stop going with the flow if that's not the direction you want to flow in.

Whatever relaxes you, allows you to re-center, takes your mind away from current events, makes you happy, or anything of that nature, is considered self care. With self care the simplest things can make you feel good and almost anything could be considered self care. What makes you feel refreshed and rejuvenated? What takes your mind away from current situations? What is self care to you? Do me a favor? Make a list of things and activities that make you feel at ease and at peace within yourself. When you are done making this list, DO IT. Don't just write about it, be about it as well. It will make you feel so much better! Also, once you begin to care for yourself as much as you care for others. you will see how you've been doing it wrong all this time.

＇

Self care is sippin' tea with my feet up,

Or A date alone to star bucks, while I watch the barista whip up drinks.

Self care is smoking Mary J while binge watching Being Mary Jane,

A nice glass of wine to stay sane,

not worrying about the time because it's 5 o'clock somewhere.

Self care is doing something new to my hair

When you look good you feel good

So make sure you take care of yourself real good

And when your cup is starting to run out,

Step back, breathe, recharge, re-center, refill.

-Garicka Jaay

That is self care to me, but what exactly is self care to you? On the next page is where you will find empty space for you to fill with your ideas of self care. Remember I dared you, so don't be a chicken. Filling this in will help you out when it comes time to schedule a self care day and you don't know what to do. You will have no excuse as to not having an idea because you have an entire list of what to do. Cross each thing off the list as you do them and once your list is completely finished, create a new one.

"Don't sacrifice yourself too much, because if you sacrifice too much there is nothing else you can give, and nobody will care for you."

-Karl Lagerfield

To me, self care is:

_____

_____

_____

_____

_____

_____

_____

_____

_____

_____

_____

_____

_____

_____

_____

_____

_____

_____

_____

_____

_____

_____

_____

Now that your list is complete, be sure to place some action behind those words. Don't talk about it, be about it and take that step forward to loving yourself a little more. When you start taking care of yourself, you will start to feel better, you start looking better, and you begin to attract better. Now, hopefully you grasped the importance of taking care of you, if not here is a quick recap:

1. Put yourself first

2. It's okay to say "no"

3. Cater to your needs

4. Treat yourself and DON'T feel bad about doing so

5. Make time for yourself

6. Stop being so available for people who wouldn't do the same for you!

Taking care of yourself is VERY IMPORTANT and should be your main priority. You can't pour from an empty glass, so take the time to step back and refill. It's okay to put yourself above others every now and then. If you aren't taking care of yourself how are you able to help them? Set boundaries and limit people's access to you. When you allow others unlimited access to you, you are disrespecting yourself. Protect your inner peace at all costs and remember self care is essential.

"If you feel "burnout" setting in, if you feel demoralized and exhausted, it is best for the sake of everyone, to withdraw and restore yourself."
-Dalai Lama

Knowing what self care is you need to understand the signs that point to you needing a self care day. We get so wrapped up in our everyday tasks that we overlook the signs that point to us needing a break. That break can last a few hours or a few days, but it's much needed. Self care is not a luxury, it's essential. Not taking the time to care for yourself can cause too much stress on your body and that's never a good sign. With some research done on the *American Institute of Stress's* website and a few observations of my own, I was able to provide a list of a few signs that point you needing a self care day.

Signs You Need a Self Care Day

- Emotionally Tired

- Feeling super stressed

- Feeling tired mentally and physically

- Feeling overwhelmed too often

- Feeling like you've got too much on your plate at one time

- Always seem to have an attitude for no reason

- Judging yourself more over simple things

- More forgetful of things, misplacing stuff more often

- Trouble finding enjoyment in anything you do

- Everything seems like a problem

- Skipping meals to get more done, so that you can squeeze more into your day

- Impatient and easily irritated

- Exhausted all the time, but have trouble sickness.

- Trouble focusing

- You seem out of whack

- Lack of interest in your hobbies and activities

These are just a few things that point to you needing a self care day. There is no need to neglect our personal needs because we would feel bad if we did so. Caring for you is a necessity that should be treated as such. Don't feel bad for taking the time out to do something that is beneficial to your physical, mental, emotional, and spiritual wellness. A self care day, or mental health day if that makes you feel less guilty, is like a recharge or breath of fresh air to those dimensions of wellness. They should become your number one priority once you realize a day to tend to your needs is needed. If you schedule yourself care dates ahead of time, you will not feel so overwhelmed and stressed out to do so.

Scheduling one day a month to cater to your needs, and your needs only, will go a long way and I'm sure you would appreciate it in due time.

We know what self care is, why it's important, and signs that we need a self care day. The only thing left is to put this information to good use and follow through. Here are 12 steps to self care that will help you on this journey straight from *MoonMemes* Instagram account with commentary from me to explain a little better. These helped me when I placed action behind them.

1. If it feels wrong, don't do it.

2. Say exactly what you mean. Don't bite your tongue when you have something to say, so save the feelings of someone else. What about how you feel? Express what you feel without feeling guilty.

3. Don't be a people pleaser. People are never satisfied. Make sure to never exert yourself for the benefit of others. Their opinion is irrelevant especially if it's going to cause you to be stressed.

4. Trust your instincts. Your instincts are like a 6th sense or a third eye, trust and believe in it because it will never lie to you.

5. Never speak ill of yourself. You should be the last person talking bad about yourself. Feed your soul positive thoughts to keep a positive outlook on yourself.

6. Never give up on your dreams. Sometimes things get hard, but don't give up. Quitting is a permanent solution to temporary problems. Write down your dreams with a plan and a date, they have now become goals. Go accomplish them.

7. Don't be afraid to say, no. Say "NO" when you want too, don't tie yourself to unwanted or unnecessary obligations.

8. Don't be afraid to say, yes. Don't be afraid to take a chance and say "yes" to new things. If you've said no numerous times, it's okay to say, "Yes" at least once.

9. Be kind to yourself. No negative talk. No talking down on yourself. Positive words only.

10. Let go of what you can't control. You can't control it so why stress over it? It's okay to not be in complete control over everything. Sometimes you just have to go with the flow.

11. Stay away from drama and negativity. Nothing comes from drama and negativity but stress, and we don't need that.

12. L O V E. Get rid of all that hatred and love, freely. Forgive others and forgive yourself, stop harnessing negative energy.

Self Care Journaling

Knowing that self care is very important let's complete this self care journaling exercise to help us achieve our goals along the way.

When do you know that YOU need self care? Everyone's "breaking" signs can be different. What signs make you say you've had enough and need a break?

When is the last time that you've scheduled a self care day or time for yourself in general? If it has been longer than a month then you need it immediately.

What is your favorite self care activity to partake in?

Schedule time for yourself, a few hours, a day, a week, whatever... Just do it. When you take the time to do so, reflect on how it made you feel to be carefree and the center of your attention. It feels good to pamper yourself and cater to your needs. It's not being selfish its self care.

"Protect your peace today, rise above any ignorance, and don't allow someone's misery to steal your joy.

-unknown

MAKING PEACE A PRIORITY

This section of self care is about protecting our peace. Protecting our peace is extremely important because peace should be a number one priority. Once you've learned to master and protect your inner peace you will be unstoppable. Once you find peace and comfort within yourself you can maintain that peace with a little practice. Finding your inner peace will help you realize how much you don't need the people who you thought, you couldn't live without. They could very well be the people who destroy your peace without recognition. Protecting your peace can shed light and help open your eyes to your current relationships and friendships. It can bring about realization of what you don't deserve and help place boundaries on behavior you will not allow in your atmosphere.

Protecting your peace is a key component in self care because if you're constantly at war with yourself and easily triggered by others, you will always feel drained. The point of self care is to learn to refill when we feel drained, if we don't protect our peace we will feel drained all the time. Your peace should be protected so good that others are angered because they can't anger you. When we are not at peace we tend to have this brain fog, seem to be on edge a lot, and make irrational decisions based off of emotions that usually lead to a lot of regret. Once you've learned to protect your peace, you will feel better in your day to day life. Your inner peace can be destroyed in so many ways and several of them are the signs of needing a self care day. Some signs that you or others are destroying your peace are as follows:

- Taking on too many tasks. This can cause you to be overwhelmed and mentally stressed.

- No alone time. I don't know about you, but sometimes I hate socializing. I am an introvert and can't stand to be interactive with people all the time. I need my time alone or I will be walking around with an attitude.

- Surrounded by negative people. You too will begin to speak and talk negatively if you are around it often.

- Responding to negativity

- Unhealthy ways of communication

- Living for others

- Harboring ill emotions and feelings toward people

- Holding on to grudges

- Company you keep

Protecting your peace, is not allowing outside people to destroy your atmosphere and mind state. This should be a goal we set for ourselves daily. In addition to it being a goal, if by chance we fail at protecting the peace in that moment, we shouldn't let that affect our mood for the remainder of the day. Don't walk around at 6pm being mad about something that happened at 8am, it's pointless. When you allow that to happen it is no one's fault, but your own because you allowed those feelings too continuously harbor throughout the day. That's how you know you've dwelled on it too much. I try to protect my peace at all times because I can't gain a piece of mind when I don't have peace in mind. My headspace will literally be everywhere. I must be at peace to make positive decisions, engage in positive and healthy relationships/friendships, to feel good about myself or any activities I'm engaging in. I have listed 13 ways that I use to protect my inner peace when I'm going through everyday situations. These ways could help you protect your inner peace or you find and develop ways that best suit you when it comes to protecting your inner peace.

1. **No Negative speaking.**

2. **Avoiding negative people**

3. **Let go of things not worth holding on to**

4. **Hold no one to their promises**

5. **Learn to not let things get to me so easily**

6. **Blocking out mean, rude, and offensive comments about myself from others.**

7. **Cancel unnecessary obligations**

8. **Watching the phone ring when I don't want to talk**

9. **Replying to people at my convenience**

10. **Choose my battles wisely**

11. **Stop being so hard on myself**

12. **Leave events and conversations when I feel like my energy is being drained**

13. **Taking time to myself to relax, reflect, and restore**

Peace is so important for me and I feel that it should be carried everywhere you go. You should not feel stressed, overwhelmed, overworked, stretched thin, angered, annoyed, or extremely emotional 24 hours a day, and seven days a week. You need some balance in your mental state to maintain a healthy and happy relationship with others and most importantly with yourself. I left you with more journaling exercises to assist you with finding and maintaining peace.

Peace Journaling

I lost my peace today because…

One way I can prevent that from happening is…

Things that bring me peace…

5 small things that made me feel at peace this week…
- ❤
- ❤
- ❤
- ❤
- ❤

My personal definition of peace is…

I feel most peaceful when I…

The most peaceful person I know is…

What/who destroys my peace?

3 ways my inner peace was challenged this week...
- ♥
- ♥
- ♥

3 ways I chose to protect my peace this week...
- ♥
- ♥
- ♥

How did I react when my inner peace was challenged?

How did I feel after I reacted the way I reacted?

What is the best thing that I have done for myself this week?

What in my life is draining my peace?

How will I remove myself or the negative energy to better protect my peace?

SELF ESTEEM

Our next step on the road to loving ourselves is self-esteem. This is built through affirming and manifesting. If you are a person who constantly needs reassurance this section will help you reassure yourself. We are our biggest critics when it comes to self. In this section, it shows you that you do not need the validation of others because you can validate yourself. Here's to the affirming and manifestation of that self love we have suppressed.

"The real difficulty is changing how you view yourself"

-Maya Angelou

Introduction

We all feel less than, at some point in our life. We go through things that can put us in a dark place mentally, encounter people who leave us in shambles, and find ourselves in situations that make us feel like we hit rock bottom. It's perfectly fine to feel like that sometimes, after all, it is healthy to allow yourself to feel. If you feel like this 75 percent of the time then this is not okay. You should not wake up every day feeling worthless or as if you have no purpose in life. You shouldn't look in the mirror everyday and think you are not beautiful like other girls or like you will never be loved. If it gets to this point, it's time we pick up our self esteem because it's definitely on the ground. When our self esteem is low for too long, it can cause you to fall into depression. Been there, done that, and I don't want to go back. Low self esteem can also cause you to make bad decisions, not live up to your full potential, and settle into unhealthy relationships. Your self esteem is your view of your value and worth, the amount of confidence you have, and how much you appreciate yourself. It's how you think you look, how you feel about yourself, what you believe, and how you act.

A person who demonstrates self love will not constantly put himself down at every opportunity that comes knocking. People who love themselves will believe in themselves, know that they are one of a kind, and pick themselves up before they have been at rock bottom for too long. It is important to have a healthy level of self esteem to carry out healthy relationships/friendships with others, give and receive love, and accomplish their goals. So ask yourself, "Is my self esteem too low?"

Self Esteem Journaling Exercise

On the following pages you'll find two quizzes. After reading each of the questions write a number beside it based on how you feel about/ relate to the question. 1 being least relating too and 5 being the most related to. Number each one honestly as you go through both sections.

Section one

1. I feel like a failure

2. I feel ugly

3. I feel like I am not pretty enough

4. I feel like I can't accomplish anything

5. I have nothing to be proud of

6. I am entitled to feel like a failure

7. I don't have much to be proud of

8. I am not satisfied with myself

9. I can never do right

10. I always mess things up

11. Nobody will ever love me

12. I put myself down

13. I compare myself to others a lot

14. I feel like a waste of energy

15. I feel bad about everything that I do

16. I am bad at everything that I do

17. I will never be great

Section 2

1. I feel accomplished most times

2. I feel beautiful sometimes

3. I am satisfied with my appearance

4. I have a lot to be proud of

5. I feel like I have a purpose

6. I try not to put myself down

7. Somebody will love me

8. I don't care if I'm loved because I love me

9. I am satisfied with myself

10. I feel like I belong

11. I am inclined to feel accomplished

12. I mess things up, but feel okay about it

13. I realize I make mistakes

14. I don't compare myself to others

15. I hardly ever compare myself to others

16. I have a good number of qualities

17. I take a positive attitude towards myself

18. I feel like a person of worth

If you answered section one with mostly 4s and 5s or section two with mostly 1s and 2s then we definitely need to work on getting your self esteem up. We should not feel bad constantly. Here are a few more questions to help us along this battle of bringing up self esteem. This will help you scrape the surface of where your self esteem issues begin to stem.

Self Esteem Journaling

How do you see yourself?

How do you think others see you?

What kind of things hurt your self esteem?

People who have hurt your self esteem?

What do you see when you look into the mirror? Are you satisfied?

When you want to feel more confident what do you do?

When do you feel proud of yourself?

In what ways do you boost your self esteem?

What are you most insecure about?

Are you happy with yourself and your accomplishments? Why or why not?

Do you beat yourself up about the mistakes you make/made? Why or why not?

If you could change something of your past to make your today better what would be?

AFFIRMATIONS & MANIFESTATION

"An affirmation opens the door. It's the beginning point on the path to change." -Louise L. Hay

Did you know what you think about daily is what you end up manifesting? Same with speaking, the way you speak of yourself is what you begin to believe. The tongue is one of the most powerful weapons you can possess. *A tongue has no bones but is strong enough to break a heart,* including your own. When you look in the mirror calling yourself ugly, you'll always believe that. You are your biggest critic and you don't need any validation from anyone, but yourself. So when you feed negativity into your soul, your soul begins to believe the toxins you place in it. Don't be one of those people who hurt themselves with nasty words, build you up. BE KIND TO YOURSELF!

I started by saying, I've dealt with insecurities from the time I was 13 until now. I have been molested by a close relative, bullied by classmates, talked about by friends, cheated on, you name it. I'm not ashamed. I'm just speaking my truth. Those situations shaped me into a shy, stand-offish insecure woman who had no idea that she was a walking masterpiece. I grew tired of not feeling like I was enough and was tired of damaging my self esteem. I picked myself apart day in and day out. I had to learn to pick myself up affirmatively. I continuously spoke positive words into the air. Affirming is all about confidently placing a positive and forceful statement of fact or belief into the atmosphere. What you put out is what you bring in. You do this by repeatedly saying a positive word, sentence, or phrase to yourself every day. When you say this, speak confidently with your head high. By doing so, you begin to convince yourself of the things you speak of. Affirmations are that reassurance you seek from others, but find within yourself. Everyone has a different opinion of you and that's okay. You have to learn that the only opinion that matters is yours. Here are a few affirmations that lifted me up from my lowest places and a few others from a close friend:

Affirmations for when you don't feel like you're enough or simply need picking up

- *"I was enough, I am enough, and I will always be enough. But I am never enough for a man who constantly wants too much".*
- *"I am the embodiment of a Goddess, anyone's inability to see that is their loss."*

- *"I am fierce and stronger than I believe; I have survived so much and can conquer even more."*

- *"Today is the day I stop saying I will try and I do, I am important."*

- *"The love I fill myself up with will break the damn that others have tried to box me in with."*

- *"I am without a doubt, that bitch and the world is mine to conquer so I will conquer it."*

- *"Nobody can be me better than me, so why would I want to be anyone else"*

- *"I will reach every goal I have set, stop doubting yourself"*

- *"I can do anything"*

- *" I am a phenomenal woman" (Maya Angelou)*

- *"My body is a projection of my soul and beliefs"*

- *"My unique skills and talents can make a profound difference in the world"*

- *My only competition is being better than the person I was yesterday or a year ago*

- *Letting my light shine will not dim others*

- *The happiness of my life is within my hands*

- *I hold a lot of love within my heart I will always give some to myself*

- *I will focus on the things I can control rather than dwell on what I cannot*

- *I welcome an abundance mindset*

- *I am and have always been a beautiful soul, my body and mind are well*

Try making a list of the things you wish to affirm in your life or a new cluster of words to help bring you up from a low place. Something you can repeat to yourself daily to help manifest into your life. When you are affirming the only way to manifest it, is to put it out there with belief. You have to believe the words that are leaving your lips. Once you start speaking it like you mean it your mind and body will follow its lead. So create you a list of the things you want to affirm and manifest into your life or a mantra to pick you up when you are feeling down. Before you make that list remember that affirmations: Start with "I AM", are specific, are short, about yourself and behavior, and most importantly they should be POSITIVE.

My List of Affirmations

-
-
-
-
-
-
-

A method a close friend of mine used to build up her self esteem was the 8 positive things activity. She had a hard time looking into the mirror without tearing herself down in the process. She embarked on herself love Journey by speaking positivity into herself daily, with the 8 positive things method. The 8 Positive things activity is where she woke up every day and found things she found good about herself. We tend to look at every negative thing about ourselves when we go through our phases of self doubt. I will not call it, self hate because we don't hate ourselves or the things, and we just tend to doubt the beauty in them from time to time.

Her advice was:

"Wake up and state 8 positive things about yourself. Look in that mirror. You are a diamond in the ruff. By stating these things you are starting off positive and you are looking directly at the root of yourself and deciding to uplift yourself. You may cry during this but this is the break through so shed those tears and remember you are worthy, you are beautiful, and you can do anything. As you stare into the mirror, smile at yourself, and say those 8 positive things. Cry if you need to, and feel the weight slowly remove itself and positivity take over more and more each day. Looking into the mirror helps you reflect directly to yourself. Always remember to embrace yourself and love yourself truly."

-C. Richardson

Another option is picking up the pieces and affirming 5 negatives into positive. This is the route that I chose to help me. I woke up every morning and over analyzed myself, *like I normally did,* but I did it with a twist. I pointed out 5 of my flaws, things I didn't like, or parts of my body I hated and spoke love to them. I found a reason to love every little thing I hated about myself through this exercise in an attempt to love them freely. I kept a journal writing everything I hated and why I should no longer hate them. Choose whichever method works best for you, whether it's speaking or writing, the 8 positives or the 5 negatives into a positive, or all of the above.

On the following pages there will be pages to help you, at least a week's worth, to get started on the methods listed above. Take the time to fill these pages in to better help you with your journey, if you'd wish to continue this method beyond the pages I've provided, start a journal to track yourself love journey and see how far you've come to loving yourself. I used a journal to keep track of the things I said to myself and how I felt, and when I say I began to notice the change it was crazy. Finding reasons to love myself no longer felt forced. I smiled more overtime and my mood seemed to have a little pep in its step! Here are the pages to begin your affirmation journal and it's an easy format to continue over into a journal of your own. Both methods were combined into one. It also combines a daily affirmation with two questions to reflect on your day. You do not have to use both methods if you don't want to. Both are there to see which method works both for you. These were helpful to me and require some consistency. Anybody can start something but can you continue to follow through with it?

Example:

Today's Date: **Today's Mood:** You can do smiley faces or words

Today I affirm: You can have the same affirmation for a week straight, a new one every day, or the same one to recite every day.

8 Positive things about me: **5 Negatives to Positive:**

1. Do this one, one day   **1.** And this one the next

2.   **2.**

3.   **3.**

4.   Or do them both each day   **4.**

5.   **5.**

6.

7.

8.

How did you feel when you woke up? (If you wake up in a bad mood what will you do to change this feeling? The world is yours and how you start your day is very important!)

At the end of today what is one thing you would like to reflect on, what is one thing you would like to begin the next day with?

Today's Date: **Today's Mood:**

Today I affirm:

8 Positive things about me:	**5 Negatives to Positive:**
1.	1.
2.	2.
3.	3.
4.	4.
5.	5.
6.	
7.	
8.	

How did you feel when you woke up? (If you wake up in a bad mood what will you do to change this feeling? The world is yours and how you start your day is very important!)

At the end of today what is one thing you would like to reflect on, what is one thing you would like to begin the next day with?

Today's Date: **Today's Mood:**

Today I affirm:

8 Positive things about me: **5 Negatives to Positive:**

1.   1.

2.   2.

3.   3.

4.   4.

5.   5.

6.

7.

8.

How did you feel when you woke up? (If you wake up in a bad mood what will you do to change this feeling? The world is yours and how you start your day is very important!)

At the end of today what is one thing you would like to reflect on, what is one thing you would like to begin the next day with?

Starting isn't the hard part, its continuously keeping the mindset to stick to the routine!

Keep going!

Today's Date: **Today's Mood:**

Today I affirm:

8 Positive things about me: **5 Negatives to Positive:**

1.   1.

2.   2.

3.   3.

4.   4.

5.   5.

6.

7.

8.

How did you feel when you woke up? (If you wake up in a bad mood what will you do to change this feeling? The world is yours and how you start your day is very important!)

At the end of today what is one thing you would like to reflect on, what is one thing you would like to begin the next day with?

Don't think of this as a tedious task, but a step in a new direction to a better way of

thinking.

Today's Date: **Today's Mood:**

Today I affirm:

8 Positive things about me: **5 Negatives to Positive:**

1.   1.

2.   2.

3.   3.

4.   4.

5.   5.

6.

7.

8.

How did you feel when you woke up? (If you wake up in a bad mood what will you do to change this feeling? The world is yours and how you start your day is very important!)

At the end of today what is one thing you would like to reflect on, what is one thing you would like to begin the next day with?

Today's Date: **Today's Mood:**

Today I affirm:

8 Positive things about me: **5 Negatives to Positive:**

1.   1.

2.   2.

3.   3.

4.   4.

5.   5.

6.

7.

8.

How did you feel when you woke up? (If you wake up in a bad mood what will you do to change this feeling? The world is yours and how you start your day is very important!)

At the end of today what is one thing you would like to reflect on, what is one thing you would like to begin the next day with?

Today's Date: **Today's Mood:**

Today I affirm:

8 Positive things about me: **5 Negatives to Positive:**

1.   1.

2.   2.

3.   3.

4.   4.

5.   5.

6.

7.

8.

How did you feel when you woke up? (If you wake up in a bad mood what will you do to change this feeling? The world is yours and how you start your day is very important!)

At the end of today what is one thing you would like to reflect on, what is one thing you would like to begin the next day with?

Wake up and have it on your mind to want better for you and place you some

action behind your words.

Today's Date:　　　　　　**Today's Mood:**

Today I affirm:

8 Positive things about me:　　　**5 Negatives to Positive:**

1.　　　　　　　　　　　　1.

2.　　　　　　　　　　　　2.

3.　　　　　　　　　　　　3.

4.　　　　　　　　　　　　4.

5.　　　　　　　　　　　　5.

6.

7.

8.

How did you feel when you woke up? (If you wake up in a bad mood what will you do to change this feeling? The world is yours and how you start your day is very important!)

At the end of today what is one thing you would like to reflect on, what is one thing you would like to begin the next day with?

I am a firm believer of speaking things into existence, law of attraction, the tongue is powerful, and you speak what you believe. Stop speaking negative to yourself and feeling yourself up with self hatred then wonder why you walk around feeling less than. Speak to yourself like you would want others to speak to you. Believing in what you affirmed will take you a long way. Once you start walking and talking like you got it, trust me, you'll have it and others will notice it as well. From the start of your day to the end, challenge yourself to speak positive words through yourself. Go that entire day, letting nothing spew from your lips, but positivity and watch how your mood differs.

The self care section taught us when we love others we care for them, and it's equally as important to love and care for ourselves. Affirming and manifesting taught us to uplift and love ourselves through speaking and repetition. When you hear things often they tend to get stuck in your head, like that one song you've had on repeat for weeks. Speaking positive to yourself provides that light in the darkness you need to make that rose grow from concrete. Speaking positive to yourself will make flowers bloom in even the darkest parts of you. When those uplifting words come from your lips, they hold so much more meaning behind them. You trust yourself more than anything so you will trust your own words before anyone else's. BE KIND TO YOURSELF, your words will also hurt you the most. Here's a quick recap from our affirmations and manifesting section:

1. Speak nice to yourself

2. Speak positivity into the atmosphere

3. Affirm for reassurance and affirm daily

4. It takes time

5. You are who you say and think you are

This next section of self esteem is about killing comparison. We have just started on building ourselves up, let's continue that process. Oftentimes, we admire the beauty of another individual and begin to wish we had *this or that* like them and we don't. That can cause insecurities to overpower your thought process. This section is about killing that comparison and why we need to leave it buried.

"Comparison is the thief of joy"

-Theodore Roosevelt

I know that girl over there is just jaw dropping gorgeous and you admire her beauty. It's okay to look at another woman and think *DAMN, she's beautiful*! What's not okay, is wishing you had this and that like her whilst putting yourself down. Don't compare yourself to her. Don't wish you were her. Don't try to change who you are to be like her. Sometimes that's easier said than done in a society who picks apart the characteristics of women saying this is how you should look. That's bullshit! Excuse my language, but its true! No one is allowed to say things like, *If she was skinnier she would be prettier, you're cute to have dark skin, or you would look better if you were thick*. Who are we to classify what characteristics qualify a person to be beautiful? Every person was created uniquely and that's something we have to remember. Theodore Roosevelt said, Comparison is the thief of joy, and I believe it.

When you begin to compare yourself to others you steal your own joy. You begin to wish you looked like them and start wanting to change yourself, meanwhile they wish they had some of your qualities. We have to learn that everyone looks differently, everyone has their own definition of beauty, and everyone has an opinion. Your opinion of yourself is ALL that matters. Don't dwell on what they have, instead illuminate your assets and qualities. You are equally as beautiful as the girl you gawk at. Of course you don't look like her, because you look like you! You couldn't pull off being her if you tried and she could never be you. You were created to be your own self and that's the beauty in it. No one can do that, but YOU! Its okay if you have previously done this, I have. There have been times where I didn't feel pretty enough because I was a shade too dark of what was "considered" beautiful. I was teased about my height, skin tone, gap, and weight through school. So I know how easy it is to want to look like the next person sometimes.

In order to love myself, I had to embrace my insecurities and grow comfortable in the skin that I am in. I built myself up through affirmations and stopped tearing myself down through comparison. I looked at myself and found the eye catching qualities that others often spoke of. I had to realize that I am a fine ass individual and one day soon the world would recognize it too. Affirmations helped me get over comparing myself to others. I'm not saying it's the complete cure because there are times when I look at a woman and be like, *"Only if I..."* What I am saying is that it's gotten me to the point where if I compare myself to someone, I kill it within the same sentence. For example: Only if I had her butt... but I've never had a problem with the one that I have.

I have provided an exercise on the following page that helped me recognize my beauty and love for myself a little more. Hopefully this helps you like it helped me. Remember to keep in mind that these changes don't occur suddenly, it takes time. Sometimes you can get so far ahead in your self love journey and relapse, that's okay. We fall sometimes, just get back up, dust yourself off, and keep going. It's hard not to compare yourself to someone, when the world around you is constantly doing it. You have to have the willpower to resist the urge to fall into that mess. That is negativity that is not needed and it begins to deter your self confidence, which begins to deter the love you have for yourself.

In this exercise, I want you to try looking at yourself through the eyes of a stranger. Take a moment to take in the beauty that is you. I mean just really take a moment to analyze the masterpiece that is you. You can do this after standing in a mirror or from memory since you do look at yourself every day. In my opinion, doing it after or while standing in the mirror really helps for the best results.

- **List five of your physical characteristics, that you think are eye catching to the people you have met. If you feel like you're having a hard time finding things I'm sure the ones that care for you wouldn't mind helping you out.**

    1.

    2.

    3.

    4.

    5.

Now that you've listed your physical qualities I want you to dig deep because true beauty also lies beneath the surface.

- **Look within yourself and find five qualities, personality traits, or characteristics that you believe are beautiful about you. This could be your personality, vibe, and caring spirit, whatever you choose. If you believe that it is something beautiful, write it down.**

1.

2.

3.

4.

5.

Here are a few more journaling prompts that are used to help you on the self esteem journey of killing comparing yourself to others. These three simple writing prompts hold a lot of meaning and will help you begin to build your self esteem. Take the time to answer these few prompts to help you along the way to our self love journey.

Describe yourself using 10 words. None of your words can be negative in any way.

1.

2.

3.

4.

5.

6.

7.

8.

9.

10.

Finish the sentences (with something positive)

If my body could talk it would say...

I feel the happiest in my skin when...

My best attribute(s) is...

I felt the best about myself this week when...

Now that you have completed the exercises do you feel any better about yourself? If these are the beautiful things that you've seen in yourself just imagine what others see in you. People have a way of seeing the things that you don't. Some of the things you hate about yourself, someone else loves about you. Do you see what I am saying? Beauty is in the eye of the beholder and baby you behold any and everything beautiful. How you treat others is also a reflection of beauty. You may have a pretty face and a nice shape, but if you treat people in any kind of way your soul is unattractive.

This section was mainly about comparing your looks to someone else, but it's much more than just looks. Comparing yourself, lifestyle, position you are currently in to the next person will drive you insane. Where they are in life has nothing to do with your current position. You don't know what they had to do to get to where they are now, you don't know that battles that they deal with or anything of that nature. You could be in a much better space than them mentally and financially and yet, you compare and kill your joy by wishing you had what they had. You're on the outside looking in and your grass could very much well be greener. You have to live for you, focus on you, and be willing to do everything it takes to get to where you want in life. Stop killing your own happiness, stop comparing yourself, stop living for others, and focus on bettering you.

We tend to feel worthless and like we have no purpose in life. We tend to be in a good space and see that someone else is much further along, and kill our confidence in the process. Everyone has a different journey and paths that they take. Focus on your own path and continue to thrive as an individual. Don't take your eye off your own prize trying to look at someone else's. These people you constantly look at should not be your competition. You're not in competition with anyone, but your old self. They should motivate you to want to be in a much better space. Don't destroy you happiness with comparison or wishing you were like the others. Gather a plan of what you want out of life and make you some goals. Accomplish them, set some more, and crush those too.

Setting and achieving goals is a good way to boost your self esteem when you feel like you are stuck at a standstill, can never do anything right, feel worthless or whatever the case may be. Set you some goals to go after and watch your self esteem begin to rise. You gain the feeling of achievement after you mark something off of your list. Our next self esteem journaling activity is goal setting. Before we set our goals we need to keep a few tips in mind so that we won't get even more discouraged along the way. When setting goals it's important to remember to:

1. Continue setting goals even if we have accomplished the ones we have set. Setting goals gives you some sort of purpose in life. It gives you something to look forward to and continue to work at. When setting goals set a reasonable time frame for some. If you have not completed the goal before the time you have set that's fine, just don't give up. Continue to work for it

and never let failure be an option. People will find reasons to quit on you every day. You have to find a reason to not quit on yourself.

2. Start small and climb your way up the goal ladder. By starting small and working all the way it boosts your self esteem. How? Well, when you aim too big too soon you get discouraged when you miss. If you start small it'll be easier to accomplish, giving you motivation to work your way up. It will give you pride in yourself, the "I can do it" mindset, and will inspire you to keep going.

3. Put some effort behind those goals you have set. You cannot expect to set goals and they accomplish themselves. You have to be willing to work at each and everyone to see the results. I know you've heard "faith without works is dead", it's true. Things will not happen because you want them to. You have to make them happen with some hard work and dedication.

4. Continue the process, keep setting goals, keep working, and keep achieving. You've got this! Now set you some goals and go crush them.

In this journaling exercise you should write out your goals and set yourself a time frame in which you would like to achieve them. If you are a person who struggles with putting effort behind things give yourself an incentive. An incentive is like a reward for reaching your goals. An incentive can literally be anything; taking you out to dinner, a pedicure, or a spa date. It doesn't matter what it is, it just needs to be something used to make you work harder. Hold up your end of the deal as well. Don't get the reward until you have completed the task. I have provided a few pages for you to set you some goals on. Write your goals, give them a time frame, and give them an incentive.

Goal Setting Journaling

Goal Setting Journaling

Remember to have a time frame and incentive

Goal Setting Journaling

Remember to have a time frame and incentive

Now that you've set your goals and your time frames, come back later to reflect on your goal setting journaling activity.

Did you achieve your goals?

If so, how many?

What was your hardest struggle when trying to achieve your goals?

How did you feel after achieving your goals?

Will you continue to set goals for yourself after this attempt at doing so?

SELF WORTH

This section is about self worth. Yes, self esteem and self worth is pretty much the same thing and are often used interchangeably. This section is about placing yourself on the throne. Placing yourself on the throne is about knowing your worth, acknowledging your worth, and refusing to settle for anything less than you deserve. This means settling for a lifestyle, relationship, or dead end job. Sometimes we forget who we are and what we are worth. It is always important to remember that. Not settling is a form of self love; you should always want the best for yourself.

"You accepted less because you thought a little was better than nothing, know

your worth"

-Unknown

SELF WORTH

Hey QUEEN, and yes I am talking to you. Our next step on our self love journey is "knowing" our self worth and placing ourselves on the throne we are more than deserving to sit on. When I say this I don't mean to place everyone else beneath you. I mean for you to recognize your worth, know what you deserve, and never settle for anything less than what you deserve. Place yourself on that throne Queen. You are beautiful, you are a talented, purpose filled individual that graces this earth and its time that you act like it. You are worthy to be here and you are overqualified. When you sit yourself on the throne you carry a certain aura of confidence. It's in your stride, your voice, and your eyes.

When we deal with a lot of situations we sometimes tend to settle for less than we deserve. Finding ourselves is a part of finding our worth. Date yourself and spend time alone. Figure out what it is that you want out of your relationships, both intimate and friendly. Realize that you deserve the best and shouldn't settle for anything less. You deserve to be cherished, not walked all over. You should be uplifted and not torn down. You should be someone's priority not there last resort. You get what I'm saying? Know your worth, place yourself on the throne, and do not come down for anyone. If they can't treat you with respect, they don't deserve to be in your presence at all. It may be hard to remove some of those types of people from your life, especially if that's all you know, but it's necessary. We hold on to toxic people and relationships because we think we won't find anything better. This is settling, don't settle. Remove whomever so that you can continue to thrive and conquer everything you want in life. Don't settle for dead end relationships, friendships, or jobs. You should be able to grow continuously with those around you. They should not be holding you back. They should be pushing you to go further than you are.

The sections we have done leading up to self worth are to help you. Yes, we are learning to love ourselves and each one of these sections could be looked back on, when we forget to love ourselves. Those sections help build you up and this section is to get you to recognize that you don't have to go back to feeling less than. We have times where we relapse, but this is here to help you fight your way back out of that space. Here are a few tips when it comes to placing ourselves on the throne,

- *Know your worth*

- *Add tax to your worth*

- *Never settle*

- *You are the catch*

- *You are a priority not an option*

- *You are the first choice not a backup plan*

- *You are equally qualified just like the next person*

- *You should be treated with respect*

- *You should always show respect*

- *You are in control of your own life*

- *You can do anything*

- *You are beautiful*

- *You are well equipped to complete anything you set your mind to*

Self Worth Journaling

What do you consider a date?

What is a deal breaker for a first date?

What is your ideal breaker for your job?

What is a deal breaker for your friendship?

What is one thing you won't do for a first date?

Something you won't do on a first date?

Things in life that you will not accept at all...

Qualities you look for in a person?

Are you scared of being alone?

How long was your last or longest relationship?

Why did your last relationship end?

Do you feel like you've gained insecurities from those relationships?

What did relationships teach you about yourself?

What did they teach you about others?

Write a list of the things you allowed in relationships that you will no longer allow:

-

-

-

-

-

-

-

-

-

-

-

Write a list of things from past friendships that you used to accept but no longer will:

-

-

-

-

-

-

-

-

-

Write your body a letter for all that it is capable of:

Write a letter to your younger self. After being in the relationships you've had, what advice would you give?

Write about a time you settled, this can be for a friendship, job, purchase, or relationship. How did settling make you feel?

It's hard to see your progress, but reflecting and being reminded that you are not where you started can be so powerful in moving someone. You should look back and applaud yourself for taking the journey and for the woman you are today and the woman you will continue to become. On these next few pages take the time to come back and reflect after you've completed it. Wait a few more weeks and complete the last reflection section. Compare your answers. You will be surprised at the progress you have made.

Self Love Reflection

Self Care Reflection

Self Esteem Reflection

Self Worth Reflection

Self Love Reflection Pt. II

Self Care Reflection Pt. II

Self Esteem Reflection Pt. 11

Self Worth Reflection Pt. II

This may be the end of the book, but it's only the beginning of your journey. Self love is never ending and it's one of the most important things you can possess. Self love lays the foundation for everything that you do in life. When you love yourself you will go after everything you deserve, push yourself to greatness, find your person and not settle because you're looking for love, and a whole lot more. Loving yourself isn't away easy, but you must continue to work at it. Remember to take some time away from everything and take care of yourself. Protect your peace and don't let anyone or anything destroy it. It's not worth the stress or energy. Affirm daily what it is in life you want, who you are, and who you will be. Be confident in yourself and don't let others opinions of you, taint your opinion of yourself.

Acknowledgments

First and foremost, thank you to the Most High for providing me with the ability to connect to others through writing and words. With love, thank you to the family who support me in everything I do. Lastly, thank you! Thank you for deciding to put forth the effort to love yourself, to maintain peace, and acknowledge your worth.

~Garicka Jaay

About the author

I was Born and raised In Muskogee, Oklahoma in 1997.

In 2010 I picked up the pen and found a peace of heaven.

I was going through hell at 11 and 12, no one ever noticed because I hid it well.

I was too closed off to communicate, so writing became my way to escape.

At age 13 my English teacher submitted my work without my knowledge and I promise I could have cursed when received a letter saying,

"Congratulations Miss Garicka Jackson! You have placed in first".

At age 16 I was sitting in computer class and my mind began to drift,

so I pulled up Microsoft word and on the screen my thoughts began to drip.

A friend of mine peaked over my shoulder and began to read my words,

She said that's exactly how she feels and my thoughts were practically hers.

At age 21 I challenged myself to break my shell,

and share with everyone the things I had to tell.

I performed my poetry at an open mic night and the way I spoke those words you could never tell that I was ever shy.

At an age 22, I performed again twice in one year even hosted my own event, I was conquering fear.

At age 23 I have hosted several shows, sharing my work with the world and accomplishing goals.

Before 2020 ended I needed to accomplish another goal,

and that was to write a book.

There's plenty more where this came from, thank you for taking a look.

Be on the lookout for more by Garicka Jaay

Subscribe on social media to stay updated.

Facebook: https://www.facebook.com/garickaj

Instagram: https://www.instagram.com/garicka_jaay/

www.ingramcontent.com/pod-product-compliance
Lightning Source LLC
Chambersburg PA
CBHW081154090426
42736CB00017B/3313